DAD Rules

Wit and Wisdom from a Dad to Whom It May Concern

Respect The Dad

[signature]

DAD Rules

Wit and Wisdom from a Dad to Whom It May Concern

Paul G. Markel © 2016

Illustrations by Design Pickle

Introduction

The material offered herein is based upon three decades of "dad" experience. While some "Dad Rules" are based upon observation, the vast majority are based upon the real-life experience of the author, me, the dad. If it seems too ridiculous to be true, it is not. Dads will understand.

My children; Jarrad, Paxton, and Zachary, unwittingly provided me with tremendous source material for this book. The reader is left to consider which story applies to which child.

Sprinkled throughout you will find short tales from the life of the author and his beloved bride. Nancy collaborated with me on the work and gave it her blessing.

"Dad Rules" is NOT a new age, touchy-feely, everyone gets a damn trophy book. There are no participation trophies in life. The sooner kids grasp that concept the better.

As a matter of fact, that is Rule #1. No one owes you anything. If you want something, get out there and earn it.

Yes, I know there are holes or missing rule numbers. Maybe I'm holding some back for later. Calm down, I know what I'm doing.

Listen, my sons, to a father's instruction;
pay attention and gain understanding.

I give you sound learning,
so do not forsake my teaching.

Proverbs 4:1-2

Dad Rule #1

In life, there are winners and there are losers. Not everyone gets a trophy. If you want something in life, you need to get out and earn it.

No one owes you a thing.

Dad Rule #2.

The thermostat, don't touch it.

That is all.

Proud Dad Moment

Dad returns home from work in the late afternoon. His little girl anxiously awaits her daddy's return.

Before dad can remove his coat, she runs up to him joyfully.

Little girl: Daddy, I can say my "s's" now!

Dad Rule #4

Do not confuse the term "rights" with "privileges". There are very few rights in the world.

Dad Tale

4-year-old son walks into father's office, father is sitting at his desk

4-y.o. son: (looks up at father) I brought two cookies from the kitchen, one for you and one for me. If you don't want yours, I'll have it.

Dad Rule #6

The next time I find 2 ounces of Kool-Aid® left in the jug because someone was too lazy to make more, the entire house will drink nothing but tap water for a month.

Don't test me.

Dad Rule #7

WANT, NEED, and DESERVE are not interchangeable terms. Beware throwing around the term "deserve", it works two ways.

Sometimes what you "deserve" might not be what you "want", but it is what you "need".

Dad Rule #9

Stop waiting around for other people to make you happy. If you want to be happy you need to make it happen.

Dad Tale

3-year-old son walks nonchalantly into the living room.

3-y.o. son: (pauses and looks at parents) Do you know what that sound was?

Mom and dad exchange glances.

Mom: No

3 y.o. son: It sounded like milk spilling in the 'fridgerator.

Dad Rule #11

'Adult Language' is a privilege reserved for adults. When you have a full-time job and a mortgage, you can say any damn thing you want to say.

Dad Rule #12

If I have to get involved in the dispute, I can guarantee neither party is going to be happy.

Police your ranks.

Dad Rule #15

Before you attempt to persuade me
by telling me that your friends
"have one" or "are all doing it", give
me their parents' phone numbers.
Perhaps they are looking to adopt.

Mom Tale

Young son is complaining about older sister cooking dinner when mom must work late.

Mom: She makes the same food that I make.

Son: Yeah, but you make it with love, she makes it with evil.

Dad Rule #16

If your mother already said no, the answer is still no. I will have to live with her long after you have moved out.

Dad Rule #17

Believe it or not, I do remember purchasing clothes for you.

Before you tell me you don't have anything to wear, take a crack at the dirty clothes reservoir behind your bed.

Dad Rule #21

Leaving 3 squares of TP on the roll
is a punishable offense.

It is indeed the same as using it all
up and is considered 'terrorism' in
many places.

Dad Rule #22

If you don't like the sandwich your mom packed for you, give it to a hungry friend. Storing a week's worth of uneaten sandwiches in your school locker is not an acceptable alternative.

Dad Tale

Mom and dad arrive at daycare center to pick up 4-year-old son.

Daycare Provider (hushed tone): We need to have a talk. Some of the boys were out on the playground sticking their middle fingers up at each other.

Mom and dad apologize and retrieve 4-y.o. from daycare.

Family are all in the car.

Dad: Did you stick your middle finger up and show it to the other kids?

4-y.o. son: Yes

Dad: Do you know what that means?

4-y.o. son: Yep, it means the 'fuck you' word.

Dad Rule #25

Take pride in your work.

Before you complete any project, regardless of the subject, ask yourself if you would be proud to have people associate your name with it.

Dad Rule #27

The person who worked a 12-hour day will decide what's on TV. I hear Best Buy is having a sale, get one for yourself.

Dad Rule #29

The Rhetorical Question is a trait
passed down from father to son.

Do I have your permission to
continue using it?

Dad Tale

Dad, frustrated in traffic, blows the car horn.

Young Son (buckled in to car seat behind him and unprompted): Asshole!

Dad Rule #33

Everyone must answer to
someone. Be glad I am just one
man, not a committee.

Dad Rule #35

It is NOT okay to use the liquid soap from the back of the sink as a replacement for the powdered dish washer detergent.

There will be a vast difference in the end results.

Dad Tale

Exasperated father overheard saying, *you're driving me crazy.*

Daddy's little girl strolls up to her father and smiles.

Little girl: Daddy, can I go crazy with you?

Dad Rule #38

There will be a 2 cookie per batch
tax instituted to offset the utility
cost for baking.

Dad Rule #40

I am glad you have an opinion. When you can back up your opinion with education and life experience, instead of feelings, I will take you more seriously.

Mom Tale

Mom walks back into kitchen where 4-year-old son is sitting at the table. Mom picks up her glass of sweet tea from the counter and drinks it.

4-y.o. son: Hey Mom, did that tea taste okay?

Mom: Yes, why?

4-y.o. son: Cuz I put dirty dishwater in it.

Dad Rule #42

Just because you 'can' does not mean that you 'should'.

You 'can' make a hot dog and ice cream sundae, that doesn't make it a good idea.

Dad Rule #44

Access to information is not the same as intelligence. Owning a "Smartphone" does not make you smart.

A chimpanzee can be taught to push buttons and play with shiny objects.

Dad Rule #46

I mowed the lawn in the summer, raked the leaves in the fall, and shoveled snow in the winter.

Please forgive me if I don't seem concerned about your "slow Internet" problem.

Proud Dad Moment

Dad picking up 7-year-old daughter from school. Daughter climbs into the front seat and buckles up.

Daughter: Daddy, when can we go shooting at the range again?

Dad Rule #47

Peeing on a tree in the woods is not the same as the tree in our neighbor's backyard or the elementary school playground.

Dad Rule #51

You can ask me a question before I have my morning coffee or after.

Please understand that my answers may vary.

Dad Rule #54

If you are eating a piece of cake off of a Tupperware® bowl lid, it might be time to search your room and under your bed for missing plates and bowls.

Mom Tale

New dog (male) climbs on young son's leg and begins humping (as dogs will do).

Young son, horrified, pushes dog away and looks up at mom.

Son: I don't have any wiener marks on me, do I?

Dad Rule #57 (sons)

If you are going to wear socks, put some shoes on your feet. Wearing socks with sandals is a privilege reserved for your grandfather.

Dad Rule #62

I may not always be correct, but I do have over four decades of "benefit of the doubt" under my belt.

Dad Rule #64

If it is in the refrigerator I bought,
it's fair game. Feel free to buy your
own fridge.

Dad Rule #76

When I offer to buy coffee, that means coffee; not a skinny, upside down, non-fat $5 Frappa-latte with cinnamon.

Proud Dad Moment

Dad and 6-year-old daughter sitting at the kitchen table. Daughter looks up at dad and smiles.

6-y.o. daughter: Daddy, if you ever get sick and your arms don't work, I will feed you.

(I fully intend to hold her to that promise)

Dad Rule #80

Life is not really all that hard.

Do what you are told. Be where you are supposed to be, when you are supposed to be there, and pick your dirty clothes up from the floor.

It's that simple.

Dad Rule #82

As intelligent people, we ask questions to gain information or to seek clarification.

If you simply want to hear your opinion repeated back to you, try talking to the mirror.

Dad Rule #88

The term "borrow" indicates an intent on your part to return said item. If you desire to keep an object indefinitely, just ask if you can have it.

Dad Rule #92

She was my girlfriend before she was your mother. You will not disrespect my girlfriend in this house.

Dad Rule #99

The family text message thread is for information that pertains to the entire family.

If you want to talk about your boyfriend, dress choices, or share silly memes please start a new private conversation.

Dad Rule #102

Unless you are a 13-year-old girl, it is not okay to leave the house with mismatched socks, ditto tennis shoes.

About the Author

An Amazon Best-Selling Author, Paul and his wife, Nancy, have successfully raised three children to adulthood.

Paul G. Markel has worn many hats during his lifetime. He has been a U.S. Marine, Police Officer, Professional Bodyguard, and Small Arms and Tactics Instructor. Mr. Markel has been writing professionally for law enforcement and firearms periodicals for twenty plus years with hundreds upon hundreds of articles and several books in print.

Mr. Markel is the host and producer of Student of the Gun TV and Radio. Mr. Markel is also the founder of Student of the Gun University, an entity dedicated to education and enlightenment.

For more information, please visit
www.studentofthegun.com

Additional Books by Paul G. Markel

Student of the Gun: a Beginner Once, a Student for Life.

Team Honey Badger: Raising Fearless Kids in a Cowardly World

Patriot Fire Team Manual

Faith and the Patriot: A Belief worth Fighting For

All books are available on Amazon.com

Also, follow us at:

www.StudentoftheGun.com

www.StudentoftheGunRadio.com

www.PatriotFireTeam.com

Made in the USA
Charleston, SC
25 January 2017